Training the best Dog ever

Lary george

TABLE OF CONTENT

1 Dog psychology

2 Toilet training for dog

3 Crate training

4 Walking advise

5 Puppy mouthing

6 Sit

7 Sleeping out of create

8 Play training

9 Socialization

10 Group training

11 Sponsor a pet

12 Understanding your puppy point of view

13. Puppy health

14 Raising your puppy in the modern world

15 Doggie daycare

16 Handling fear

17 Grooming

18 Sleeping schedule

19 How can I keep my baby safe with my dog

1 Dog psychology

Dogs may communicate their emotions through their mouth, eyes, ears, and tail. They can converse with people, which is one of the reasons they make excellent pets.

Your puppy's facial expressions may make you smile or squeal, but their expressiveness extends far beyond the way they look.

Talking to your dog will be simpler if you are aware of their body language.

Nothing compares to welcoming a brand-new canine into your house and heart

2 Toilet training

It's crucial to praise and encourage your puppy right away when he or she successfully uses a designated area or a toilet pad. Your puppy will pick it up quickly because they pick things up quickly:

Most of our adult dogs will already be trained to use the bathroom, but they might need some reminders. Take them outside into the garden when you first get home and wait there until they have relieved themselves. Give them calm compliments when they leave.

Whether you're getting a puppy or an adult dog, toilet training is a crucial component of providing responsible care for your pet. You must be knowledgeable about proper house training techniques. Puppies must learn crucial life lessons,

You'll quickly learn that pups urinate frequently—sometimes more than 12 times each day! Your responsibility is to lead them so they don't blunder, determine when they need to go outside, and instruct them on what to do when they get there. Of course, you should also give them praise when they get it correctly.

3 Crate training

Dogs are inherently den creatures, and the majority of them prefer being in small, confined spaces, despite the fact that many people see crates through the human perspective of being "caged up." When taught to utilize them from an early age, crates can help reduce anxiety because they give animals a sense of security.

Place the crate in the family room or another place where the family spends a lot of time at home.

Drop some tiny food goodies nearby, then just inside the door, and ultimately all the way inside the crate to entice your dog to enter.

Young puppies shouldn't be left in their crates for more than two to three hours without going potty.

4 Walking advise

Giving your dog some basic commands will help you stop negative behaviors around the house, such as item theft. Shoes, kid's toys, and other items with strong scents are commonly taken by dogs.

You don't need to demonstrate to the dog that you are the "boss" or "pack leader" because these ideas come from outdated training techniques that have been demonstrated to be useless.

If your dog behaves in the other way and collapses to the ground, changes direction abruptly, or is otherwise easily frightened

Even though it's not always the easiest task, teaching your dog appropriate behavior in public is possible. It's crucial to understand when and how to give your dog rewards.

Making the most of your dog's time while out on a walk is one of my favorite dog walking ideas, and the simplest way to accomplish that is to let them explore.

5 Puppy mouthing

Although mouthing is a safe method for puppies to explore the world when they are small, as they get bigger, it can start to feel like biting, therefore it's crucial to start teaching them not to mouth at a young age.

Puppies use their mouths and their razor-sharp teeth throughout all of these common activities. Puppies frequently bite, chew, and mouth on people's hands, limbs, and clothing while they play with them.

It's crucial to break your puppy of the behavior early on because as they get older, mouthing becomes even less desired and begins to feel more like biting.

You can anticipate when your dog will act out by keeping a daily journal of their activities. If you can foresee the times of day or situations that could set off the mouthing,

6 Sit

of their age, any dog can be taught to sit! This activity can be learned by puppies as early as six weeks old, and older dogs with normal mobility can also pick it up.

In order to avoid intimidating and confusing your dog, never press their back end down. Additionally, give the treat to your dog when it is sitting to encourage that position.

The actions a dog decides to take in the absence of a cue from their owner or another handler are known as default behaviors.

7 Sleeping out of create

You've had success keeping your dog in the cage at night or while you were at work, but now you want to move him into his cozy dog bed.

Even though your tiny Labrador is still a pup, they have enough energy to keep you up all night. The children adore spending time with your new animal family member.

8 Play training

There are many goals when it comes to training your

 training challenges your dog and ultimately makes them smarter.

Your dog needs to understand what you anticipate from them in order to get off to a good (and paw!) start with them. They will feel more confident as a result that they can achieve the set objectives moving forward.

9 Socialization

Your puppy will go through a socialization phase during their first three months of life that will permanently influence their personality and how they respond to their environment as an adult dog.

To assist your puppy develop accustomed to all kinds of sights, noises, and smells in a pleasant way, socializing is the idea.

Inadequate socializing might cause behavior issues in later life.

There are many socialization activities you may engage in before your puppy has finished their vaccines, whether inside your home or by going on puppy-safe "field trips," as socializing is not just about your dog encountering other dogs and humans.

10 Group training

The first session may seem like a nightmare, whether your dog is pulling erratically toward the other dogs, acting as though she's never met you, barking as the instructor speaks, or hiding beneath your chair. You might even be tempted to claim that this is actually your neighbor's dog and that you are merely helping out.

If your dog is extremely excitable while meeting new dogs, group classes may seem like a terrifying concept because of the possibility of meeting a variety of canines. Similarly, if your dog is timid or jittery, you could feel uneasy about enrolling them

11 Sponsor a pet

All the love and care you can give is what the animals in our shelter need. Although you might not be able to adopt right now, you can always Sponsor A Pet to let other people who might want to adopt this animal know that it is special enough to be sponsored!

12 Understanding your puppy point of view

Let's say an adorable, 8-week-old puppy decides to move into your home. Your home might have a lot of incredibly strange items in it or a lot of things that are familiar from your puppy's perspective. What your puppy was accustomed to throughout the first few weeks of its life will determine how it will react.

Keep a watchful eye on your dog's actions. Keep an eye out for subtle as well as more evident answers. You may tell by your dog's replies how receptive they are to new interactions with people or other canines. You'll be able to tell by other replies if your dog is relaxed enough to learn.

13 puppy health

One of life's greatest pleasures is being able to hug and cuddle a gorgeous, cuddly dog.

A key component of appropriate puppy care is understanding puppy nutrition. Because of how his or her body is developing, your puppy's quality of life will be affected for many years to come.

It is strongly advised against giving your puppy food from your plate. Many times, puppies will ask for whatever you are eating,

You should choose a food made specifically for puppies rather than older dogs because your puppy's body is developing in crucial ways.

14 Raising your puppy in the modern world

Although puppies are utterly gorgeous, raising one comes with many difficulties. The task at hand can seem very overwhelming if you've never had a puppy before, but once those large puppy eyes steal your heart, it gets easier.

Although they don't always sleep through the night, puppies sleep a lot. The good news is that your puppy may awaken the household by whining and barking to express their displeasure at being left alone. As their adult teeth erupt, puppies are also motivated to chew a lot. As a result, puppies may discover the canine equivalent of a teething ring in your favorite pair of shoes, the rug in your living room, or even your hand. It's crucial to keep in mind that raising a puppy is a short-term task if you start to get dissatisfied with your new pet.

We are aware that persons who have previously owned a puppy tend to do better during socialization and training. From their prior experience, they have gained knowledge.

15 Doggie daycare

Short-term daytime care for dogs is referred to as dog daycare or doggy daycare. It is distinct from pet sitting and extended kennel boarding.

Even if you don't plan on going back to work right away, you should consider how your pet will be cared for when you are not home. Dogs should never be left alone for more than four hours, and puppies should only be left for about an hour at a time.

To stop the transmission of contagious illnesses and parasites, all dogs in daycare facilities, whether they are private or public, must be in good health. Owners of dogs are required to show documentation of their dogs' most recent vaccinations.

16 Handling fear

Make an attempt to massage your dog's head or neck and speak in a calming tone when they are nearby. Make a big deal out of your dog when they come running up to you in the park; this will encourage them to want to be close to you more.

Perhaps this entails taking your dog for walks at times of day when you are less likely to encounter whatever the dog is scared of (other dogs, unfamiliar people, etc.).

17 Grooming

Your dog will feel and look his best with proper grooming. Regular grooming appointments also provide you a chance to check your dog's coat, teeth, eyes, ears, and nails for any indications of health issues. The size, breed, and kind of coat of your dog will determine how frequently you should groom him.

It might not be possible anymore to take your dog to get groomed, or you might still feel safer keeping your dog at home. In the comfort and familiarity of your own home, it might be simpler and less expensive for you to take care of your dog's basic grooming requirements.

18 Sleeping schedule

You must develop a daily routine, including feeding, walking, playing, and sleeping patterns, in order to keep your puppy healthy and obedient. This post will go over the ideal puppy sleep pattern and how much sleep puppies need as they become older.

A common misconception among new dog owners is that their puppy naps excessively. In an effort to help the pet "sleep better at night," they wake it up on purpose during the day. Some people wake them up to play or pet them.

Puppies expend a lot of energy when they are awake because they are physically developing, discovering new people and places, and discovering what they are capable of. Considering how fascinating and entertaining the world is,

19 How can I keep my baby safe with my dog

Never leave an infant unattended on the floor with a dog in an aggressive mood; dogs can move swiftly even if you are sitting next to them.

Parents should get comfortable offering cues in all positions. For instance, lying in bed, sitting on the floor, or reclined on a couch. When you are resting in different positions and your dog does not listen to commands like "sit" and "down," you will need to train him so that he will always comprehend.

In a safe and controlled atmosphere, socialize your dog with kids.

Keep an eye out for how the dog tries to get your attention.

Don't wait until the baby is born to enforce any new rules you have for your dog, such as keeping them off of furniture or out of specific rooms. Particularly if those things weren't off-limits before, your pooch needs some time to acclimatize.